CREATE IT!

CUBIST ART

Alix Wood

 Gareth Stevens
PUBLISHING

Thank you to
Davina Cresswell
and Jemma Martin
for their help with
this book.

Please visit our website, **www.garethstevens.com**. For a free color catalog of all
our high-quality books, call toll free 1-800-542-2595 or fax 1-877-542-2596

Cataloging-in-Publication Data

Names: Wood, Alix.
Title: Cubist art / Alix Wood.
Description: New York : Gareth Stevens Publishing, 2017. | Series: Create it! | Includes index.
Identifiers: ISBN 9781482450392 (pbk.) | ISBN 9781482450415 (library bound) |
    ISBN 9781482450408 (6 pack)
Subjects: LCSH: Cubism--Juvenile literature.
Classification: LCC N6494.C8 W66 2017| DDC 709'.04'032--dc23

First Edition

Published in 2017 by
Gareth Stevens Publishing
111 East 14th Street, Suite 349
New York, NY 10003

Copyright © 2017 Alix Wood Books

Produced for Gareth Stevens by Alix Wood Books
Designed by Alix Wood
Editor: Eloise Macgregor

Photo credits: Cover, 1, 7, 8 bottom, 9, 10 bottom, 11, 13, 14, 15, 17, 18, 19, 23, 27, 28 bottom, 29 © Alix Wood;
3, 4, 6 top, 12 middle, 20 bottom, 21, 24, 25, 28 top © Dollar Photo Club; 6 bottom © Collection of Mr. and
Mrs. Paul Mellon; 12 bottom, 16 bottom © Shutterstock; 20 top © The Eugene and Margaret McDermott Art
Fund, Inc; 22 bottom © Triton Foundation; 26 © Artothek; all remaining images are in the public domain

Printed in the United States of America
CPSIA compliance information: Batch #CS16GS: For further information contact
Gareth Stevens, New York, New York at 1-800-542-2595.

CONTENTS

WHAT IS CUBIST ART?

Artists often like to find new ways to paint things. Otherwise, art might all look a little bit the same! Cubists tried to find new ways to paint **three-dimensional** (3-D) objects on a flat piece of paper. Some Cubists solved this problem by painting strong shapes such as **spheres** and **cubes** that seemed to pop out of the page.

Other Cubists drew objects from different angles at once. In this painting, the people's faces are looking straight at us, but their mouths are drawn viewed from the side.

Meet a Cubist Artist

Paul Cézanne (left) is sometimes thought of as an **Impressionist** artist. However, his work inspired the Cubists that came after him. He liked to paint strong shapes, like these round peaches.

A detail from a painting by Cézanne

TECHNIQUE TIPS

Cubists started using **collages** in their art. Collages are pieces of art made by sticking materials such as photographs, pieces of paper, or fabric onto a backing.

a collage

PAUL CÉZANNE

Paul Cézanne painted using solid 3-D shapes in many of his paintings. Cézanne believed everything in the world was made up of either a cube, a sphere, a **cone**, or a **cylinder**.

cube   sphere   cone   cylinder

Cézanne's Houses in Provence

CREATE IT!

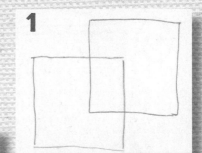

Try drawing a 3-D house.
You will need: paper, pencil

1 To draw a cube, draw two same size squares. The second square should be up and to the right of the first.

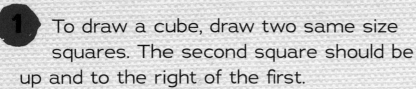

2 Draw a line connecting the top right corner of one square to the top right corner of the other.

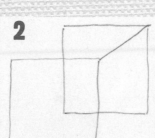

3 Join the other corners to their matching corners.

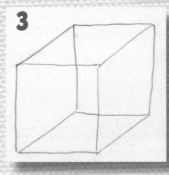

4 Erase some of the lines to make a cube.

---

1 To draw a roof shape, first draw a horizontal line.

2 Next, draw two lines at either end, leaning right at the same angle.

3 Draw a line to form the top of the roof. Draw an angled line down for the side of the roof. If you draw the cube and the roof together, you have drawn a house!

Try drawing some 3-D fruit like these apples and lemon by Cézanne.

You will need: paper, a pencil, pastels or chalks, some round fruit such as apples, plums, or grapes.

1 First, practice drawing round 3-D shapes. Draw a circle. Decide where your light is coming from. Using the side of your pencil, gradually shade the shape. Get darker as you shade farther from the light source.

light source

2 Choose some fruit to draw. Arrange the pieces how you want them. If you really squint your eyes, you can see the dark and light areas more easily. Try it.

3 Draw your shapes in pencil. Color the bottom of each piece of fruit using pastels or chalks. Gently smudge some of the pastel with your finger up to the top half of each fruit.

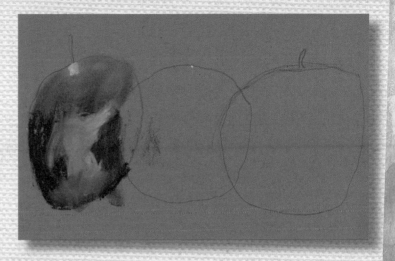

4 Add a little white highlight. Add some darker shadows using a tiny smudge of black.

CREATE IT!

Now you can draw a house, so try creating a village like the one above by Cézanne.

You will need: paper, a pencil, watercolor paints or watercolor pencils, a paintbrush

1 Draw your houses first using pencil. Pay attention to the solid shapes, such as cubes, that make up your houses.

2 Using watercolor pencils or paints, start to color the background. Watercolor pencils turn into paint if you go over the marks with a wet paintbrush.

3 Now color in the houses. You can leave some white if you like. To make the houses look 3-D, color their sides a darker shade than the fronts.

GEORGES BRAQUE

French artist Georges Braque liked Cézanne's paintings. Braque was interested in strong shapes. He became an important Cubist artist.

Braque often painted birds such as the dove in his painting *The Messenger*.

TECHNIQUE TIPS

Braque would often break his picture up into shapes. In this painting, Cubist artist Vaclav Taus has drawn a pear and a glass using Braque's style. He has shaded each shape to look 3-D.

CREATE IT!

You will need: paper, pencil, watercolors

1 Choose a simple object and draw it on your paper using a pencil.

2 Now draw lines all over your paper. Overlap your drawing too.

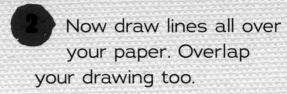

3 Color the shapes in your object using shades of its real color. Color the background in shades of another color.

4 Use a pencil to outline the shapes and lightly shade them to look 3-D.

PABLO PICASSO

Pablo Picasso was a famous Spanish artist. He was friends with Georges Braque. The two Cubist painters often painted together in each other's **studios**. They would help and encourage each other.

This stamp shows Picasso's Cubist portrait of his partner Françoise, and their children Claude and Paloma.

Two Faces

When Picasso painted people, he would often paint their face from the front and the side all in the same painting! In this way he made a flat piece of paper more like a sculpture!

S.TOMÉ E PRÍNCIPE

17

Françoise, Claude e Paloma, 1951

1881 – CENTENÁRIO DE PABLO PICASSO – 1981

CREATE IT!

You will need: paper, a pencil, a black marker, colored pencils. If you can, take a photo of yourself from the side. You can look at the photo to help you draw your **profile**.

1 Using a pencil, draw just the outline of your face, looking straight on. Then draw your face viewed from the side, down the middle of your drawing.

2 Now add your other eye, the other side of your mouth, and hair, all viewed from the front this time.

3 Color in your picture, and add a colorful background.

CREATE IT!

You will need: colored paper, a pencil, colored pastels or chalks, scissors, glue

1 Using a pencil, draw the outline of your head. Don't draw any features on your face yet. You will draw and stick those on later.

2 Using the pastels or chalks, color your drawing in. Use blocks of bright colors.

TECHNIQUE TIPS

Pastels and chalks can be very messy. Color from the top of the paper down, otherwise you may smudge your drawing with your arm.

18

3 Draw your eyes, nose, and mouth onto pieces of brightly colored paper. Color them in.

4 Try placing your features on the drawing to see where they look best. When you are happy, glue them onto your drawing.

JUAN GRIS

Spanish artist Juan Gris is sometimes called "The Third Cubist." Picasso and Braque are the best-known Cubist artists, but Gris is well-known too. He often used collage in his artworks.

Gris' painting *Guitar and Pipe.* Can you find the pipe?

CREATE IT!

You will need: some color magazines, paper, scissors, glue

1 Look through some color magazines and find three pictures that you like. Choose images that might look good together.

2 Cut your chosen images into interesting shapes.

3 Arrange your shapes onto a sheet of paper. Glue them in place when you are happy with your design.

GEORGES VALMIER

Georges Valmier was a French Cubist painter. He painted portraits, **still life**, and also designed sets and costumes for the theater and ballet.

Valmier's Portrait of Commandant Lambert

TECHNIQUE TIPS

In Valmier's *Portrait of Commandant Lambert*, Valmier makes him look as though he is made of blocklike shapes! See if you can draw a portrait using 3-D shapes.

CREATE IT!

You will need: paper, a pencil, watercolor paints

1 Look at the face you are drawing. Does it seem square, or round, or diamond-shaped? Draw 3-D shapes that best match what you see.

2 Use interesting colors for your background. Try shading your 3-D shapes using light and dark shades.

CREATE IT!

Georges Valmier liked to create collages in his art.

You will need: printed photographs or pictures from magazines, paint, a paintbrush, construction paper, scissors, glue

1 Print out some photographs of your family, or find some pictures of people from magazines.

2 Check that it is okay to cut up your photographs. Cut them into interesting shapes. Mix up the sizes and the angle of the features to make a fun collage.

3 Paint a fun background on construction paper. This will be the background for your collage. Let it dry.

4 Arrange your collage until you are happy with how it looks. Then glue the pieces in place.

FERNAND LÉGER

Fernand Léger was a French painter, sculptor, and filmmaker. He created a form of cubism. His bold, simple paintings of modern life inspired a later art style known as **Pop Art**.

Art critic Louis Vauxcelles poked fun at Léger's style by calling it "tubism"! This was because Léger often used cylinder shapes in his paintings. This 1916 painting, *Soldier with a Pipe,* has lots of tubes.

Can you make out the figure of the soldier and his pipe in this painting?

You will need: paper, a pencil

1 Try drawing cylinders. First, draw two, similar-sized, oval shapes next to each other.

2 Draw two lines to join the oval shapes at the top and the bottom.

3 Erase the left-hand side of the right oval. Now your shape should look like a 3-D cylinder.

4 Decide where your light is coming from. Shade your cylinder on the side farthest from the light.

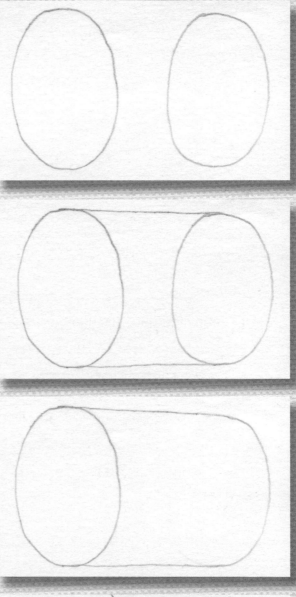

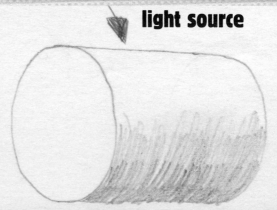

light source

CREATE IT!

Try drawing a person using cylinders.

You will need: a pencil, a ballpoint pen, paper, paints or colored pencils, a paintbrush, an eraser

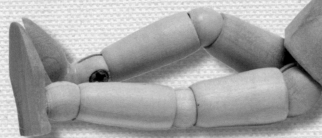

1 Using pencil, draw a stick man. Draw a line for his head, neck, and body. Draw lines for both halves of his arms and legs, too.

2 Imagine your stick man is made of cardboard tubes, joined together with string. Draw cylinders where each body part would be.

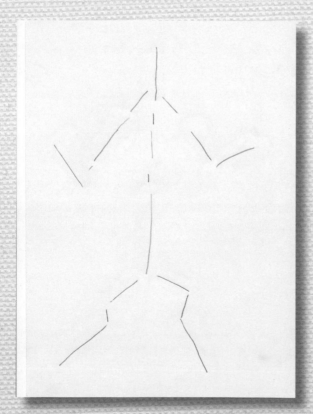

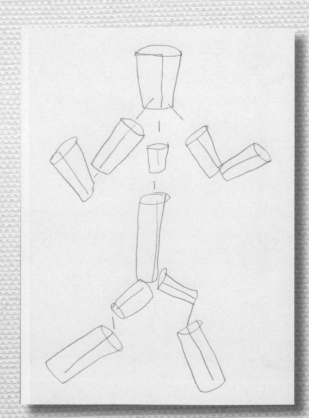

3 Using a ballpoint pen, draw over your cylinders. Erase any pencil lines you no longer need.

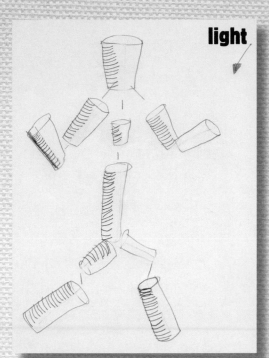

light

4 Decide which side the light is coming from. With your ballpoint pen, draw lines to shade the side farthest away from the light. The shading looks best if your lines follow the curve of the cylinder.

5 Color in your cylinder man using paint or colored pencils.

TECHNIQUE TIPS

You won't have to shade your cylinders with the paint. The shading you have already done will make the cylinders look 3-D.

art critic A person who writes his or her opinion about art.

collages Works of art made by gluing pieces of different materials to a flat surface.

cone A solid figure that slopes evenly to a point from a usually circular base.

cubes Solid shapes that have six equal square sides.

cylinder A geometric shape of two identical parallel circles and a curved surface that completely connects their borders.

Impressionist An artist who practices a style of art in which the subject is not as important as how the artist uses color and tone.

Pop Art A form of art that depicts objects or scenes from everyday life and uses techniques of commercial art and popular illustration.

profile A head or face seen or drawn from the side.

spheres Objects that are shaped like a ball.

still life Pictures of objects that are often carefully arranged by the artist.

studios The working places of artists.

three-dimensional Having height, width, and depth. A flat picture, such as a photograph, is two-dimensional. A sculpture is three-dimensional.

Books

Bloess, Willi. *Milestones of Art: Pablo Picasso: The King: A Graphic Novel.* Vancouver, WA: Bluewater Productions, 2013.

Venezia, Mike. *Paul Cezanne (Getting to Know the World's Greatest Artists (Paperback).* New York, NY: Children's Press/Franklin Watts, 2016.

Websites

Ducksters site with information about famous cubist painters and their work:
http://www.ducksters.com/history/art/cubism.php

Tate Kids website with a fun game based on Cubism:
https://kids.tate.org.uk/games/cuboom/

Publisher's note to educators and parents:
Our editors have carefully reviewed these websites to ensure that they are suitable for students. Many websites change frequently, however, and we cannot guarantee that a site's future contents will continue to meet our high standards of quality and educational value. Be advised that students should be closely supervised whenever they access the Internet.

INDEX